CUP

PRINCETON

DOG OBEDIENCE TRAINING

Ross Allan

I am particularly indebted for the help of my wife and closest friend Margaret, an outstanding dog trainer in her own right.
Photography by Merlyn Lange.
I wish to thank the following for their most valuable assistance with the illustrations: Margaret Allan, Christopher Allan, Jeffrey Allan, Aleisa Allan, Ryan Kitzelman. German Shepherd - Jaimon Qdette. (Daisy) German Shepherd - Kleersky Utes Sioux C.D.X. (Nikita) German Shepherd - Nickaris Calendar Girl. (Cassie) German Shepherd - Freestien Eclipse. (Robyn) German Shepherd - Pallendon Quattro. (Quattro) Golden Retriever - Antanas Gold Champagne. (Charmayne) Rottweiler - Fiorella Black Orefo. (Beau) Border Collie cross - Tazz.

DEDICATION

I dedicate this book to my father and mother, Leo and June Allan, and to the dear memory of my late mother-in-law and father-in-law, Thora and Dave Lawler.

TRIBUTES

I wish to take the opportunity to pay tribute to R.A.A.F. Cpl. Nev Kershaw and the officer in charge of the original NSW Police Dog unit, the late Sgt. Jack O'Reilly. These people displayed a talent with dog training so incredible that they became legends in their own lifetimes. Whilst I have never met the two gentlemen, the stories of their feats inspired me as a young dog handler and still do.

Sgt. Bruce (Farmer) Stevenson, who was the biggest influence on my dog training attitudes and standard.

Ruby Smith and her late husband Alf—my mentor in the trialing arena.

Australian television programmes "Burke's Back Yard" and "Talk to the Animals." Both excellent programmes that have advanced the dog world in Australia light years since their inception.

I also extend the greatest appreciation to Almighty God and Dr. Herbert R. Axelrod for giving me this opportunity.

yearBOOKS,INC.
Dr. Herbert R. Axelrod,
   Founder & Chairman
Neal Pronek
   Chief Editor
Andrew De Prisco
   Editor

yearBOOKS are all photo composed, color separated and designed on Scitex equipment in Neptune, N.J. with the following staff:

DIGITAL PRE-PRESS
Michael L. Secord
   Supervisor
Robert Onyrscuk
   Computer Art
Sherise Buhagiar
Patti Escabi
Sandra Taylor Gale
Pat Marotta
Joanne Muzyka

Advertising Sales
George Campbell
   Chief
Amy Manning
   Director
Jennifer Feidt
   Coordinator

©yearBOOKS,Inc.
1 TFH Plaza
Neptune, N.J. 07753
Completely manufactured in Neptune, N.J.
USA

Selecting the right dog obedience training book has become as difficult as choosing the right dog breed. There are hundreds to choose from written by many qualified author-trainers. Ross Allan is an exception. He and his family are fully immersed in the training of dogs. Ross understands the dog's mind and can relay his knowledge to his readers with captivating ease.

This yearBOOK on DOG OBEDIENCE TRAINING proudly sets forth Ross Allan's practical training techniques. He does not pretend to teach you to train your dog to jump through a loop of fire, instead he introduces the basics of dog training in straightforward, simple language that any beginning dog owner can understand.

What are yearBOOKS?

In order to get up-to-date information out to the general public, yearBOOKS,Inc. is publishing books in magazine format. This means lower prices because of the support of generous advertisers and the less expensive way magazines are manufactured.

Because this information is so valuable, a hardcover edition, sewn for longevity, has also been made available.

The Foto-Glaze™ used to enhance the beauty of the color photographs is protected by U.S. Patent 5,249,878.

ACKNOWLEDGMENTS

Space does not allow me to acknowledge all the people who have played a large part in my dog training life, however it is with great pleasure that I now have the opportunity to thank the most prominent R.A.A.F. personnel as follows, bearing in mind that the ranks may have changed—Group Captain Tom Meldrum, Squadron Leader Bill Perrett, Flt. Sgt. Tom Daly, Flt. Sgt. Kev Saunders, Sgt. Lance Robinson, Cpl. Kev Mahon, Cpl. Mal Holland, Cpl. Nev Kliedon, LAC Jeff Woods, Sgt. Royce Cooper of R.A.A.F. Police.

I also wish to thank a number of people who gave unselfishly of their time or support, and without whose outstanding efforts I would not have been able to bring my business out of a crippling debt, thus enabling me to survive—Tony Mckee, Mick Heaney, Pam Fischer, Elaine Gough, Monica Stewart, Peter, Evelyn and Angela Brinkworth, Tony Morgan, Barry and Alex Hunter, Stan and Barbara Bourgoure, Keith Graham, Robert Gazler, Fred Humphries, Hideto (Harry) Imamura, Noriyoki (Neville) Shinozaki, Kay Jones, Lal and Mark Trenery, Robin K. Scantlebury, Gary (Pancho) Cron, Lindsay Miller, Gary Sorenson, Graham Martin, Wayne and Jenny MacDonald, Eddie Fenton, and the members of the Capricorn Coast Obedience Club. Mark Crosby, Peter Ruhle, Ryan Kitzelman, Tracey Ohl and Ross Davidson for their evaluation of my book and training procedures.

Also for the valuable advice received from Pamela Odijk, author of *Writing for Money,* and her husband Herman.

CONTENTS

**PHOTOGRAPHY BY
MARGARET ALLAN.**
Additional photographs by
H. Odijk and K. Taylor.

INTRODUCTION

I was most fortunate to learn my field of dog training in the R.A.A.F. at a time in its history when it was the biggest and most advanced dog training centre in Australia and was recognised internationally. Bill Perrett, the founder and Officer in Charge of the Mustering for 25 years, was a leader in the insistence of controlled attack-trained dogs. Indeed, whilst other much bigger military services in other parts of

Don't try this at home. Proving the superiority of the Alsatian, this R.A.A.F. performance dog is in top form.

The author Ross Allan demonstrating the fire ring jump with a star German Shepherd pupil.

the world were beating their dogs off agitators with big sticks to make them leave off an attack, the R.A.A.F. dogs along with the London Metropolitan Police Dogs were performing this task on voice control of the handler.

Upon graduating from the Police Dog Training Centre, Toowoomba QLD, it was to my great advantage, I later learned, to have been a novice in the world of very experienced dog handlers, some of whom were particularly gifted in this area. No matter how well I trained my dog in certain exercises, there was always someone around who had done the same thing better. In effect I had served a four-year apprenticeship which proved invaluable in instilling in me the view

that the only real expert on a dog is the dog itself, and I'll never really be anymore than the dog's student.

I'm often asked by obedience trialing people the difference between the R.A.A.F. training and obedience training. And, whilst I have to go back 20 years to reflect on my experiences (as I've never kept in contact with the Mustering), there were numerous differences as R.A.A.F. dogs were working dogs and trained for reliability irrespective of weather, terrain or any unforeseen circumstances, whereas trialing is a sport.

The most distinctive

The author poses with one of many German Shepherd students.

difference that regularly comes to mind is the attitudes of the respective trainers. The R.A.A.F. handlers in my time were very positive and confident and never blamed anything or anyone but themselves for an exercise problem with their dog. Perhaps a

Understand your dog and praise him. A strong bond between dog and owner guarantees more success in training. This is the author in 1972 with R.A.A.F police dog "Pal."

big help to this end was the extensive basic training in dog psychology. Once a person has a good understanding of the mind of a dog they only have themselves to blame for a training problem, and realising this, set about correcting it in a methodical manner. Laziness is the curse of a dog trainer.

It is the work ethic and importance of basic dog psychology that is the focus of this book. This content

can help any person who is interested in problem solving or training a dog to be reliable in obedience and a credit to its owner as well as being a well behaved member of the community.

Daisy and Ross sharing a tender moment. Sitting pretty comes easy to Daisy.

About the Author

Ross Allan was born on the 9th of May 1949 at Jandowae, QLD, Australia. He was educated in bush schools in the Tara area until his parents moved to Barrack Heights, NSW, where he finished his schooling at nearby Kiama High. Ross's attraction to dogs surfaced as a toddler, much to his mother's concern as he was often bitten on the face as a result of running up to strange dogs and giving them an enthusiastic hug.

The author's affection for the German Shepherd and dogs in general can be traced to the famous "Rin Tin Tin." This is Robyn.

The author's interest in dog training was stimulated by the "Rin Tin Tin" television series, and by consuming the numerous books available those days from public libraries about police and military man-dog teams.

Ross's first dog was a Border Collie-cross male called Taza which he acquired when he was 12 years old. He trained Taza to perform a large array of tricks and in his own words, "the dog must have trained itself because I never had much idea what I was doing. I just contributed a great deal of time and effort, and most importantly I guess, I adored the little fellow. And he rewarded me."

The author joined the R.A.A.F. in 1969 as a trainee medical orderly, then remustered to general hand when he opted off the course. His postings landed him at Williamtown, NSW, where he first discovered the Police Dog Mustering. A subsequent friendship with Greg Meldrum, the Commanding Officer's son, led his father, Group

Captain Meldrum, to fight officialdom and gain Ross entry into the Police Dog Training Centre, Toowoomba, QLD.

The author graduated in 1970 with honours as "Dux of course" and "Trainer of the Top Dog of Course." Six months later Flt. Lt. Perrett, OC of the Mustering, conducted his annual assessments throughout Australia, Singapore and Malaya, and awarded Ross and Police Dog Pal third place.

Mr. Perrett's annual

This is the author's wife Margaret Allan with Charmayne, a Golden Retriever puppy.

The author has had hands-on training of over two thousand dogs of a variety of breeds and temperaments for the general public in the area of obedience, protection and tracking. He is also an assistant instructor at the Capricorn Obedience Club, Yeppoon, Queensland.

The author is ably assisted by his wife Margaret, sons Christopher and Jeffrey, and daughter Aleisa.

When your dog trusts you, there is very little he will not allow. Hands on training can affect many lessons faster than vocal commands.

assessments the following year found the author and P.D. Pal awarded the prestigious "Perrett Trophy" for "Top Man-Dog Team, Royal Australian Air Force 1972."

The author left the R.A.A.F. in 1975, continuing to train dogs on and off until 1984 when he set up a training complex at Struck Oil, Mount Morgan, QLD, initially assisted by Bill Perrett, then retired.

FOREWORD

Ross Davidson
Ambulance Officer
Public Education Officer
Rockhampton District
As a young teenager in the late 1970s, I formed an

ambition to join the R.A.A.F. Police Dog Mustering, motivated by the high level of training and the numerous highly acclaimed public displays at that time.

The R.A.A.F. Police Dog Training Centre was regarded as the best dog training institution in the country. It was so highly regarded in this field that other services such as police forces and military and prison services were originally trained by the R.A.A.F.

My ambition continued into my late teens and I often made inquiries, pestering recruiting officers at every opportunity with a view to joining this elite group of people. During my conversations with older R.A.A.F. dog handlers and recruiting officers, there was one name that shone above all others. This name was mentioned with such esteem and vigour that it was hard to believe that the person was real. The name was Ross Allan.

Over the last 12 months of high school I hounded the recruiting officers for further information to assist in compiling a school project on the Mustering, and Ross's name would be mentioned countless times during this time. I found he and his partner Police Dog Pal had become an integral part of the R.A.A.F. Police Dog Mustering history.

Although Ross had been out of the Police Dog

Training dogs for the Allans is a family affair.

Mustering for ten years, I made a promise to myself that one day I would meet this man who appeared to be a legend amongst his peers. I was later elated to find that Ross Allan, the name that had graced the corridors of the R.A.A.F. Police Dog Mustering for over a decade after his retirement from the service, had established a dog training school within my locality. Ross was ably assisted by his wife Margaret.

I made it a point to meet this living legend of the R.A.A.F. and I am delighted to say that I was not disappointed in doing so. Over the years I have spent endless hours with Ross in both the dog training and social bounds. Ross has a quiet, unassuming nature and his willingness to listen to others, no matter at what level, is a trait of his I admire.

Those who know Ross see him as a devoted family man and a person with a very determined nature. His reputation within the dog training industry for

training the "untrainable" dog spans the country. Ross builds an incredible bond with all the dogs he trains. His patience, dedication and rapport with the animals he trains is nothing short of remarkable.

The magic aura that surrounds Ross when he speaks about dog training is like a magnet to the novice and experienced trainer alike. Although I might add he would rather listen than talk and I find this aspect of his character most unusual in the dog world.

Ross sincerely regards himself as a student of dog training. I have never known him to ever put himself in a category in which I and many others regard him as—an expert. Again, in my view, this is one of many of Ross's finer qualities. There have been occasions when Ross and I have been in the company of others who were discussing dog training. Later, I have said

to him, "you don't agree with what they were saying, why didn't you tell them you believed they were wrong?," and his reply is always the same, "everyone has a right to their opinion. And I'm not God's gift to the dog world." It is this attitude and positive nature that puts Ross in a class of his own.

With the publishing of this book, I feel that the recognition that Ross deserves will finally emerge. I have seen firsthand the amount of energy that he generates when training, locked into the dog with a concentration so intense that he completely shuts out the rest of the world.

I am also proud to have trained a very difficult dog using the methods in his book and achieved great success. Ross is a true inspiration to all dog

Author's son Jeffrey with Quattro. Jeff and his brother Christopher and sister Aleisa ably assist Ross with his obedience school.

trainers across the country and a patriarch to the dog training profession. I count myself amongst his closest friends and hope that others may prosper from his teachings.

INTRODUCTION TO  TRAINING

This book is designed to offer a practical training programme for the beginner without bogging him down in academic waffle or offering false promises. It is much easier to supervise people with their training than it is to teach through the pages of a book. Whilst there are a number of good obedience and Schutzhund clubs providing competent supervised training courses, many people find it difficult to attend classes due to distance or other commitments on allocated training nights.

This programme is meant to be seen as open and flexible, and although a day-by-day schedule is mapped out, it is meant only as a guide covering the six basic obedience exercises: heel, sit, stand, drop, stay, and recall (come when called). It must be understood that it takes many months to train a dog to a very high standard so that it is totally reliable under most circumstances. The handler will make mistakes during this period; indeed highly experienced trainers continue a learning spiral if they are honest with themselves.

Experienced trainers are usually training a number of dogs over a period of time and each dog is an individual with its own personality, intelligence level, and idiosyncrasies. Consequently, trainers have to be flexible people who can adjust to each individual dog. Due to the fact that each dog is an individual it has to be trained accordingly. It takes experience and experimentation on the part of the handler to eventually find out what works best for their dog. For example, some dogs need to be trained daily for a good response, others respond better to a few days training and couple of days rest. Some people achieve quicker results than others and this can be attributed to the fact that some people have more ability to train dogs than others, or some dogs may be more trainable than other dogs. Some dogs, who may not be as intelligent as others, may have a stronger inherent desire to please than most. Hence, their training improves comparatively quickly.

Regardless of whether one is training a dog simply to be a working dog in some field such as police, prison, security, military work, etc., or just to be a better member of the family, the bottom line is to train a dog to be reliably obedient under most circumstances. The purpose of this book, therefore, is to introduce the reader to basic dog psychology and the rudiments of teaching the dog basic obedience exercises. I wish to point out at this time that many authors of dog training books and magazine articles go into great detail in an attempt to convince the reader that his/her book offers the best method of training, and that all other methods are outdated or inferior. My experience is that most methods offered have some merit. However, I am of the opinion dog training is highly individual and this individualism should be encouraged.

Whilst I believe that handlers should be constantly on the lookout for ways to assist and improve their expertise in this field, I suggest that those experienced in dog training and who have had considerable success should change their methods with caution rather than get swept up in some new trendy method that is, from time to time, promoted as the "new" dog training programme. I feel one must bear in mind that there have been and still are many trainers in obedience and working fields that have quietly achieved incredibly well-trained dogs through an understanding of basic dog psychology and a healthy application of common sense.

Before getting into the nuts and bolts of obedience training I shall first explain some basic psychology.

Generally the dog is still basically a primitive animal even though it has adapted to our lifestyles, and that feat in itself is remarkable when one considers that people have enough trouble living with one another—so it must be hard on a lot of dogs (e.g., most dogs are natural scavengers and this is exhibited by their love for decaying road kills, their fondness for rolling in foul-smelling objects to disguise their scent, males marking their territory and so on).

The most important aspect of the dog's thinking that concerns us when training them in obedience exercises is the fact that they are pack animals. The dog running in the wild with a pack quickly learns that there is a pecking order and unless it has the superior strength and ability to defeat all the other

members of the pack, it will find itself relegated to its level of physical superiority within the ranks. Dogs also adopt their position within the human ranks when living with family.

For example, dominant male dogs in a normal

Praise and eye contact are essential in any training programme.

family environment are usually more respectful of the husband, less so with the wife and, whilst friendly with the children, will rarely do as they tell him. Whilst I believe that dog training should be viewed as a pleasant and enjoyable exercise, it must be appreciated that some dogs can be very hard to train and well-intentioned efforts can be fraught with frustration.

All dogs do not come from the same mould and usually they are not particularly obliging

during the course of this type of training. Some dogs, I hasten to add, are extremely difficult to train and would test the skills of the most proficient trainer.

Dogs are basically primitive animals, do not do obedience-type exercises in the wild of course, and they really don't see much point in doing it for you. However, a well-adjusted dog with an affectionate and loyal disposition will quickly learn to enjoy his new-found lifestyle and, whilst being a little unco-operative at times, will enjoy his training sessions. Moreover, consistent, sensible training of the dog will make his world one of black and white, not shades of grey. He will be taught what he is allowed to do and not allowed to do. He should no longer be punished for things he doesn't know he has done wrong, because the trainer will learn through the following pages how to understand his dog.

Dogs are living, breathing, emotional creatures of independent mind.

To generalise I will break the types of dogs into three categories:

Type 1: *Good to train.* Well adjusted, loyal, devoted and generally not a problem and, best indication of all, comes when called.

fences, etc. Strange as it may seem, this type of dog is often labelled as stupid by the owners when in fact it is usually highly intelligent, and like a hyperactive child they get bored easily and hence turn to mischief.

If the dog is shy or timid, he requires more patience and a gentler hand than an outgoing, confident dog does.

Type 3: *Shy timid dogs.* Dogs born this way may prove very difficult to train.

Also dogs who have been ill-treated may exhibit traits of great fear or may even be aggressive. However, with a great deal of patience and commitment they may train well.

Before digging into our practical training we will look at a few training principles. *Please read the book completely before commencing training.*

Type 2: *Very hard to train.* This type is an arrogant, stubborn sort and may be male or female. They may be very friendly to friends and burglars alike, or indeed, very aggressive toward people outside the family and other dogs. The male dog is a macho type and his attitude is usually governed by an excess production of male hormones. If you are training these type dogs you should consider castration—discuss the possibilities with your veterinarian.

These dogs may also be very subservient, fawning and crawling, conveying the impression of being very loving on one hand, but in fact they exhibit infuriating habits such as not coming when called, running away every time the gate is left open, continually jumping

Never underestimate the importance of spending quality time with the animal you are attempting to train.

BASIC TRAINING
PRINCIPLES

REPETITION

Dogs learn and remember by exercises being conducted in a repetitive manner. That is, the dog is continually caused to repeat the basic exercises over and over until they are so firmly planted in his brain that the exercises become automatic. Please remember that should you slacken off the training the dog will become rusty so don't expect it to be as sharp and cooperative as it was when trained regularly. Dogs also develop memory blocks and unintentionally regress in exercises from time to time, proving that regular repetition does not cement all exercises for evermore. Our memory as people fade if we stop doing something for a while, so why shouldn't a dog's memory fade?

PRAISE

Praise with the benefit of voice or hand is used to reward the dog but unfortunately, is often most lacking from trainers. The dog should be praised whenever it has done an exercise correctly, or if it has been corrected, the dog should be praised

indicating to the dog what it must do. The golden rule of praise, regardless of it being given by voice or hand, is sincerity. Dogs aren't fooled by insincere or patronising praise and are as unimpressed as a beautifully groomed woman given a condescending compliment from a patronising man. In short, be sincere or keep your mouth shut. The dog is being trained as if it is on

Four Paws Quick fit muzzles are the most comfortable and humane muzzles for dogs. Allows dogs to drink water while wearng the muzzles. Made of nylon and completely washable. Photo courtesy of Four Paws.

the level of a toddler so praise must be warm, friendly, affectionate and genuine.

I don't use profuse praise and bounce around excitedly with the dog when it completes an exercise correctly—I find that it distracts the dog and causes it to lose concentration. Should the dog sit on my command, I lift up its face with my left hand, pat it under the chin and around the ears, look directly into its eyes—still in the sit position—and speak several words spoken in a warm, affectionate tone, making the dog feel comfortable and relaxed. I should point out that I do make use of gay, profuse praise when teaching the dog exercises such as retrieving, jumps, finding articles etc., but these exercises are not covered in this particular book.

I rarely make use of food as a reward, but rely on the importance of bonding closely with the dog, encouraging it to adore me. I do not disapprove of the use of food as an enticement to teach a dog who is being difficult with an exercise; e.g., a type 2 dog being a problem not cooperating with the drop exercise may go down with food as the inducement. But I believe the food inducement

affection the dogs are happy. Whilst I do not object to the occasional food treat during training I believe that the bottom line of obedience is that the dog must be taught to do as it is told, when it is told and to do so without reward other than to please the trainer.

The dog seeks to read your mind by looking directly into your eyes. Eye contact can speak louder than commands.

BONDING

If ever there was a secret to successful dog training it would have to be the aspect of bonding or developing a rapport with the dog. I have often witnessed a trainer take a dog of average ability and convert that particular dog to a work of art in the areas of obedience, protection, and tracking.

Certainly dogs with an abundance of natural ability train much faster, but to train a less able dog to a high standard takes a trainer who not only has enormous patience and determination, but the ability to reach deep into the dog, bringing out a love and devotion so strong that the trainer is the dog's sole purpose for living.

To take the title of an outstanding television programme as a well-worded example, "Talk to the Animals." Always find time to have a chat with your dog, play a game, a lay on the grass, a cuddle in

should be dropped within a few days of achieving success and the dog taught to work because the pack leader (trainer) wants it that way.

I do, however, object to the practice of recent years where dogs are taught to be gluttons by continual feeding. In this case, the trainer is basically bribing the dog into performing exercises like a circus animal. A number of dog handlers competing in obedience trials are conditioning their dogs to come completely alive at the prospect of food, thereby presenting an artificially alert appearance. The resulting picture of a bright happy dog is designed to impress an obedience judge with the fond hope of gaining extra points. This dog is taught

that if it pays close attention to the handler it will get a food treat, and not to work because it loves and respects the trainer (pack leader). Indeed, if the trainer has made it a point to develop a strong bond with the dog it will work to please and need no other reward.

As I stated previously, I rarely use food as a reward, but I do occasionally use it as a training aid. However, I much prefer to see a dog in deep concentration working with its handler even if the tail is not wagging and the ears are down. The dog is exhibiting its natural demeanour (dogs do have differing personalities from bright and smiling to dour and serious just like humans), and as long as the handler gives freely of praise and front of the television, or take it for drives or good long walks. Make your dog one of your closest and dearest friends.

CORRECTIONS

Corrections may vary from a stern word, a check with a lead, to a sharp smack on the rump. Remembering that a dog is basically a primitive animal, it understands a pecking order in the pack. If a dog steps out of line in the pack it is chastised swiftly and firmly in a no-nonsense manner. Errant puppies, of course, are very quickly punished by mum and taught their place. In this case the trainer must establish himself as the pack leader in the eyes of the dog.

Voice intonation or inflection is probably the most valuable training aid and is very important in reprimanding an offending dog to put it in its place. Likewise it is valuable in praising a dog to reward it and make it feel good.

Voice correction with type 2 dogs will be much firmer than with type 1 dogs, with type 3 dogs often not being

reprimanded at all.

Voice correction, like praise, must be sincere. If the dog commits a mild offence then a mild scolding is warranted. If the offender exhibits a determination to be particularly arrogant then the trainer will need to use sharp, harsh voice correction. Should the dog be particularly pigheaded, the trainer can bring the sky down on it with his voice by giving it a loud blasting using numerous words delivered in a most angry and hostile manner.

The correction words may be "no," " naughty," "bad," or "behave." It really doesn't matter—it's the tone of the voice that counts.

The check or choke chain and lead serve as a useful correction aid with the

check chain over the dog's head and around its neck, lead attached and trainer holding the lead in the right hand. A forceful correction can be given by the trainer to the offending dog by snapping the lead sharply across its body, which is particularly required with type 2 dogs. The trainer's left hand remains free to reposition the dog in its exercises and also to pat the dog in order to praise it.

The left hand is also used to give the dog a sharp cuff on the rump at times as one would correct a toddler (I didn't say bash the dog). Again the force varies from dog to dog, type 2 dogs needing a forceful no-nonsense hand at times, and type 3 no smack at all due to their timid nature. Remember the hand that

Excellent training aids to keep dogs away from forbidden areas of your garden are available through pet supply stores. Most of these deterrents can be used indoors on furniture and rugs or outdoors on flowerbeds, shrubs, and garbage cans. Photograph courtesy of Four Paws.

smacks is the hand that pats and as long as praise is given generously at all times the dog will not be hand-shy.

All corrections must be carried out immediately after the dog does something wrong not only in its training, but also in day-to-day matters.

The golden rule is that *it is better to be too soft than too hard*. The handler can always come down harder on a dog if it's getting away

When you make a rule don't enforce it one day and not the next. For example, if the dog is to sit and wait before being allowed to eat its meal, don't sit it some times and not others. The dog must be made to sit every time or not at all. The dog should never be given a command unless the trainer is prepared to enforce it. To illustrate, take a situation where the trainer is relaxing on the

chair and put the dog back where it was originally told to adopt the drop position—or say nothing to the dog in the first place.

NO POWERS OF REASONING

Dogs do an incredible job coping in a human environment, given the complexities of the human nature. But obedience exercises can be confusing to the dog unless we grasp the fact that dogs can't always read our minds, nor should they ever be expected to.

Give your dog a cuddle while laying on the grass . . . spending time with a dog establishes a rapport of trust. Christopher and Jeffrey Allan spend time with Daisy and Tazz.

Take for instance the dog that is being trained per the obedience trialing system of exercises. The handler walks along at a given pace directed by a judge with the dog at the heel position by the trainer's left side. The judge then instructs the trainer to drop, stand or sit their dog as they come to a halt. If that is the only way the dog is taught to perform these exercises, it will not normally perform these three exercises up and down by the handler's side whilst the trainer remains in the halt position. If the dog is taught to perform these three exercises as per the trialing system, and to sit, drop, and stand by the

with too much, but it can be very hard to build up a dog's confidence if it has suffered corrections too severe for its temperament.

CONSISTENCY

It is vital that the dog's world be converted into one of black and white and this is mainly achieved by being consistent with the dog's training and its general behaviour.

back patio with friends and the dog wanders onto the patio and walks towards the trainer. If the trainer happens to command the dog to drop, the dog must lay down where the trainer gave the command. If the dog wanders around to the far side of the trainer and lays down, that is not good enough. The trainer must be prepared to get up out of his comfortable trainer's side whilst he is in the halt position, the dog will not usually perform them should the trainer leave the dog in a stay position and stand in front facing the dog, then command the dog to adopt sit, stand or drop positions. Each series of exercises has to be taught separately to the dog because it simply doesn't understand what is required due to the nature of the work involved. The only thing that limits a good dog's training—be it obedience, guarding, tracking, obstacles, herding, or whatever—is the trainer's own imagination.

Don't be afraid or embarrassed to talk to your dog.

It helps to remind yourself to pretend that you are working with the equivalent of a toddler whenever a new exercise is commenced and break the training down to the simplest steps. It is paramount that the trainer always bear in mind that for the purposes of training, *the dog has no powers of reasoning.*

EYE CONTACT

The dog seeks to read a person's mind by looking directly into his eyes. The dog seeking communication with the trainer will not look at his feet or chest; he will stare intently at the trainer's eyes, so clearly that we must use our eyes to communicate with the

dog. Staring at a strange aggressive dog can be interpreted as a threat by the dog, but this not the case with a pet. It is a fact that if trainer and dog have a very close bonding, the trainer can put the dog in a stay position, leave it walking several paces away, then turn and face it. The trainer can then focus on

the dog, concentrating intently and looking directly into the dog's eyes. The trainer can hold the dog's full attention for several minutes if necessary before breaking contact. This little exercise takes practice and is difficult with a dog until it matures, but it can be done. Dogs who will not make good eye contact are very difficult to train.

ATTITUDE

Whilst training the dog, always concentrate on the task at hand. The trainer must learn to switch off the day's events, relax, and focus on the issue in hand; that is, the training of the

dog. Never train a dog if you are in a bad mood. Settle down first, take the dog for a long walk, have a play with it and settle yourself down before training. Whilst a good temper tantrum can work wonders to remind a type 2 dog who the pack leader is, the temper tantrum must be a good act so that the trainer can switch back to the role of companion.

LOOK IN THE MIRROR

If you have a good dog and you're having problems with it, look in the mirror— *it's your fault.*

Admittedly there may be dogs classified as type 2 and 3 who may be beyond training in obedience. These dogs require an enormous amount of dedication and patience on the part of the trainer, and in the case of type 2s, a very determined nature. Facts must be faced and some dogs are simply square pegs in round holes. It may be better to consider placing the dog

your dog. The trainer will have to go over some exercises literally hundreds of times before the series of exercises are cemented in the dog's mind. This programme is mapped out as a guide in order to get the average dog to a good standard of obedience; in fact, it can take much longer to achieve a high standard depending on the ability of the dog and the ability of the trainer.

This book is designed to get you started remembering the importance of repetition, for even if a dog has been trained to a high standard of obedience it will get rusty and forgetful if the training is not kept up.

Play is as important a part of training as are the basic commands. The Nylabone® Frisbee™* (with a bone implanted on top) is the safest and most fun for dogs. This Frisbee™*, made especially for dogs, can be picked up easily and will bear the dog's chewing without fraying and cracking.

*The trademark Frisbee is used under license from Matell, Inc., California, USA.

PATIENCE

People fortunate enough to own a type 1 dog will never have their patience fully tested. The owners of type 2 and 3 dogs are a different story. Type 2 owners can expect to be desperately struggling to manhandle a large male dog that is determined to check out a park or fight another dog, or a medium-

appropriately, particularly in the case of a working dog breed cooped up in a town yard, when its place is clearly in the country.

A golden rule generally is: if the trainer is having a problem teaching the dog an exercise it is usually the trainer's fault. The communication line has broken down, *so think for*

sized bitch slithering on the ground fawning and crawling around the trainer's legs, pretending to be cute and cuddly in a pathetic attempt to avoid the trainer's wishes.

The trainers of type 3 dogs take it in easy stages and can expect to make slower progress than types 1 and 2. Indeed, nervous, timid dogs can take up to 18 months to reach a sound all-around standard, although progress can be observed at an early stage and the results for the type 3 trainers are particularly rewarding.

Determination, commitment, and persistence are equally important virtues. Trainers of all types will have to accept that successful dog training is a long and repetitious project and the prerequisite for a good trainer is patience and determination.

REGULAR TRAINING

It is imperative that time is set aside most days of the week even if it is only for ten minutes a session. The trainer can not catch up on lost time—if he misses two or three days an extra-long session later will not make up for lost time. Constant

Indirect training is as important as a special training session in the park. Showing her good manners, Charmayne is waiting for permission to eat.

handling is most important and a short training session squeezed into a busy day's routine is far better than skipping it altogether.

REST PERIODS

Dogs need a break to help absorb the training. Their brains can be overtaxed just like humans and suffer from stress even to the extent of a nervous breakdown. They also get bored if they are over-trained.

INDIRECT TRAINING

This is as important as a special session in the park. Examples include making the dog sit and wait for meals, sitting and staying before entering the car,

A fine example of indirect training: here Cassie is waiting for Ryan's permission to enter the car.

sitting and waiting until after the chain is removed or being allowed out of a kennel, drop-staying beside the trainer's chair for close companionship, practice-calling the dog (recalls) whilst the dog is running around the yard, practice sits, drops, and stands during commercial breaks on the television, and many others. In fact, any opportunity that presents itself can be used to an advantage to strengthen the dog's training.

REVERSE LOGIC

Before commencing practical training the trainer must understand that pin-pricking the dog's positioning in the exercises

is necessary. As humans, when we do a job we hate someone standing behind us continually pin-pricking our work. We know that if a task is explained well, we like to be left alone to get on with it. However, in dog training we cannot explain what we want the dog to do and not to do. We have to physically pull and push the dog around to put it in various positions, remembering to reward the dog with praise until it clearly understands what we want of it. For example, the ideally correct sit position for the dog beside the trainer would have the dog situated beside the trainer's left leg facing forward, parallel to the trainer's body with the dog's chest level with the front of the trainer's legs. Now, we could spend the next ten years putting the dog in this position, however, the dog would not

know it could not sit with its backside behind the trainer, or away from the trainer until it is corrected and positioned correctly.

Dogs, being animals of independent mind, will always test the trainer as a child will a parent—dogs are great compromisers. For example, when the trainer positions the dog in the sit, it will invariably attempt to sit incorrectly for quite some time (not straight and parallel). The dog is saying, "All right, I'll sit, but I'll do it my way." Trainers cannot compromise; we are talking about discipline and the dog must do as the trainer desires. Remember, once the rules are set the trainer must be consistent.

SOCIALISATION

From the time the dog is immunised so that it is protected against deadly diseases common to dogs, it should be taken out and about so that it gets used to all sorts of environments and situations, such as parks, fields, roads, shopping centres, people patting it, car and other animal noises and smells, etc.

A well-socialised dog will be relaxed in almost any environment and easier to train. However, some people form the misguided view that a dog they wish to use for protective purposes should be kept away from all people so that it will be suspicious and aggressive to everyone. Not only is this act more likely to have the opposite effect (causing the dog to lack confidence and become fearful of new situations), but it can develop into a fear biter, becoming a danger to the community in general.

The owner should condition the dog to be a confident, well- balanced dog first, then consider keeping it away from strangers to strengthen its protective role if it is considered necessary.

MEDICAL CONDITION

Dogs can suffer from physical conditions that may cause training problems. Illnesses such as cancers, brain tumors, etc., can sometimes explain the behaviour of a problem dog. If in doubt have the dog checked by a veterinarian.

COMMANDS

Commands can be given by voice or hand signals. Voice commands given verbally not only serve the purpose of communicating to the dog that an action is required from it in response to a particular spoken word, but the voice tone can reprimand or praise the dog at the same time with the command. For example, if a dog begins to get sloppy when the trainer tells the dog to sit, the tone of the command could be

somewhat harsh. Alternately, if the dog is working well the command sit can be given in a pleasant tone.

Change the tone and pitch of each individual command so the dog learns a particular tone to each command. For example, the trainer says "sit" in a set way and every time the

Guaranteed by the manufacturer to stop any dog, any size, any weight from ever pulling again. It's like having power steering for your dog. Photo courtesy of Four Paws.

command sit is used, the same tone and pitch is used. The trainer may say "sit" making the word short with high tone, while the drop command may be short and spoken in a low tone and so on. The dog then learns a second set of commands and should the occasion arise where the dog misses the actual word it recognises the tone relating to that word and obeys regardless.

Commands should be given in a moderate tone— not loud. Dogs have very sensitive hearing—about six to eight times better than ours. Therefore loud commands should only be used when the dog is becoming ignorant and needs a verbal reminder to behave itself.

The dog should be trained by giving verbal commands in a moderate tone of voice in a distinct inflection for each exercise. As the training progresses the commands should be given in a softer tone so that the dog has to concentrate more closely on the trainer. With the dog trained to obey softly spoken commands, the trainer can then raise his voice and adopt a harsh no-nonsense tone to smartly reprimand the dog with great effect if required.

Commands are single word commands; i.e., not "sit down," "lie down," or "come here," but "sit," "drop," and "come."

HAND SIGNALS

A specific hand motion can be made to the dog at the same time a voice command is given. Different hand movements may be used for individual

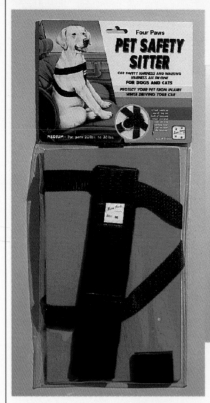

exercises. For example, whilst the dog is walking along at the heel position by the trainer's left side, the trainer can command the dog to stop walking and remain in a stand position by giving the command "stand" and at the same time making a semicircular or windshield wiper motion in front of the dog's eyes with the right or left hand.

Initially, hand signals must be given directly in front of the dog's

face so he clearly sees them. As time goes on and the dog is alert for hand signals they may be given somewhat above the dog's head. Dogs have very clear upward vision due to the lack of a forehead, subsequently allowing the dog to easily detect movement above its head.

Use only one command word for each exercise. If a second command is used it must definitely be the last; then make the dog obey. To continue using the command is not only nagging the dog but also confusing it. Keep it clear and simple for the dog: one command for heel, sit, stand, drop, come, and stay—not "heel heel heel" or "sit sit sit," etc.

TRAINING EQUIPMENT

The equipment required to train the dog is simple—one good quality check chain that allows about 4 inches (100mm) of slack after it is fitted over the dog's head and a lead constructed of good quality leather, $^{3}/_{4}$ of an inch (19mm) wide and 5 feet (1.5m) to 6 feet (1.8m) in length, with the end looped over large enough to slip the hand in and out freely, with a good quality snap or clip stitched at the other end. One piece of metal rod, such as a tent peg, will be necessary to restrain the dog in long stays & recalls, along with a light rope about 20 feet in length with a good quality snap or clip at one end.

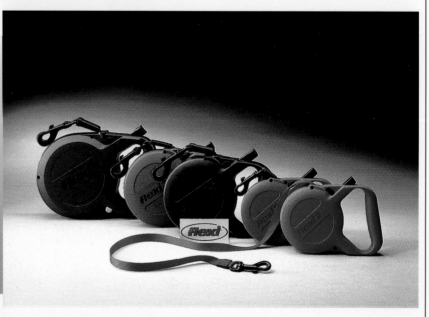

BEST AGE
TO TRAIN A DOG

A brilliant book was written many years ago by an American gentleman, Clarence Pfaffenberger, called *The New Knowledge of Dog Behaviour*. Pfaffenberger's book supplied scientifically researched information invaluable to the dog world.

Pfaffenberger was involved with the training of war dogs used by the American armed forces during World War II, and then employed by the Guide Dogs for the Blind, Inc. (San Rafael, California) to improve the breeding and training programme for this centre. At this time Pfaffenberger combined his research with Dr. J.P. Scott, who had started research into the study of puppies to learn about child behaviour. This study took place at the Roscoe B. Jackson Memorial Laboratory, Bar Harbor, Maine.

The subsequent findings of the research by both of these incredible gentlemen was so thorough that it would seem to be impossible to be improved upon. The end result for the Guide Dog centre was that it went from turning out a 9% success rate of trained guide dogs to a 90% success rate.

Some interesting facts emerged which are relevant to the trainers of dogs in the obedience area, such as:

1. Puppies do not begin their learning process until three weeks of age;
2. By seven weeks of age the puppies' brains are fully developed and are like little computers waiting to receive information;
3. From seven to

This is Charmayne at 15 weeks. Puppies at this age can become rebellious and attempt to defy their owners. Be patient and consistent through this testing period.

16 weeks they are going to learn the things that will mould their characters as adults;
4. If they are not taught by their human masters during this time they will find a way to learn other things on their own.
5. Between the ages of 12 weeks and 16 weeks puppies usually go through a stage similar to our "tantrum two's."

In their own little way they become rebellious and defy the pack leaders—the owners in our case. For example, generally puppies housetrain very quickly until they hit 12 weeks; then they start soiling inside for no apparent reason for a period of time before they continue to housetrain again. Similarly, many puppies will regularly come when called until they hit this period, then suddenly develop a case of deafness. Parents who have raised toddlers will understand this growth phase with tantrums and screaming sessions from their own experience.

Pfaffenberger and Scott determined this particular period as the time the owner must establish pack leadership with the puppy.

My experience has

A dog's positive mental outlook is intrinsically connected to his need to chew. Providing a Gumabone® for your dog keeps him occupied and his teeth healthy and clean.

Scott clearly ascertained that puppies as young as three weeks can start their learning process—e.g., conditioned to being handled by people, becoming sociable with humans, getting used to a variety of experiences, noises, smells, etc. Indeed puppies as young as six weeks can be taught basic obedience exercises and in fact, I've tested puppies 11 weeks old in basic tracking exercises with amazing results.

I recall experimentation I was conducting for Det. Sgt. Ian Lane, formerly of the Drug Squad, Newcastle, NSW., in relation to canine marijuana-detecting capabilities. At this time I was in the R.A.A.F. Police Dog Mustering stationed at Williamtown. Ian subsequently used the results of these tests and other information obtained from the R.A.A.F. to submit an application for the reintroduction of the NSW. Police Dog Unit. The year was 1972 and the use of drug detection dogs in the country was still in its early stages. During the course of these experiments I trained a German Shepherd bitch puppy called "Taffie" to detect marijuana. I commenced the training at seven weeks of age and she was successfully finding the drug at 12 weeks of age.

As for the maximum age to train a dog, I've yet to find one. As long as the dog enjoys good mental and physical health it can be taught basic obedience to a very good standard at an old age, providing that the trainer takes the age of the dog into account and exercises some old-fashioned common sense.

A physiological problem common to male dogs around the three- to four-year mark occurs causing a change in behaviour. This change is usually in the form of the dog becoming intolerant with children and sometimes a distinct body odour becomes apparent. This problem is quickly rectified by a trip to the veterinarian and appropriate treatment.

further shown that the second most important training phrase was between 16 weeks and six months, and the most difficult time with most breeds was between six months and two years. I would suggest that dogs go through a development stage similar to our teenage years before maturing.

I'm not saying for one moment that dogs between six months and two years can't be trained; of course they can and also train very well. Pfaffenberger and

PUPPY TRAINING

Puppies should never be bought as a toy for a child. Children are usually rather rough with animals even with the best of intentions, and puppies are living, breathing, emotional creatures who not only suffer physical pain but also the ill effects of mental cruelty. Children should not be allowed to drag the puppy around the house, sit on it, push little fingers into its eyes or ears, etc.

Children should only be permitted to handle and play with puppies under parental supervision. Unfortunately many a good dog has been put to death because its patience was exhausted from the effects of suffering cruel treatment at the hands of children.

Where possible a sleeping puppy should never be disturbed. Apart from the fact that a puppy is a baby and needs its sleep, constant handling at these times can cause a puppy to develop into a hyperactive dog.

PUPPY TRAINING

As I mentioned earlier, puppies commence learning at three weeks of age, so

> **Puppies can be introduced to formal training from eight weeks of age. Don't expect too much until the puppy is about five months of age. Here Charmayne is doing a stay.**

the breeder or owner of the puppy should begin the handling at that age. A few minutes a day of simple things like nursing the pup and talking quietly to it is sufficient.

Puppies become most receptive by six weeks of age and they can be taught the basic obedience exercises. By limiting the training to just a few minutes at a time the trainer can tell the pup to sit, then hold its head up with one hand and push its behind down with the other whilst praising at the same time. The same is done with the stand and drop exercises with the puppy held in position initially for two or three seconds. As it learns to associate the command and the position it is placed in at the same time, the period of time can be slowly extended over the coming months.

The short training sessions can take place several times a day with the trainer standing in front of the puppy, beside it, or even whilst the trainer is seated on a chair. Remember—only a few minutes at a time.

The puppy hits the equivalent of our "tantrum twos" at about 12 to 16 weeks and will start becoming defiant in its own little way. It is at this time, we are told, that a little challenge for pack leadership is on. No problem—the trainer

Puppies benefit from early training. Acclimating the dog to obedience training from an early age can only help to mould the dog's behaviour patterns.

simply becomes more determined in the training sessions.

It is very important that the recall exercise (coming when called) is introduced from the time the puppy seeks human company. This is simply introduced by making a big fuss of the puppy when it seeks the trainer's company,

regardless of the area—whether it be in the house, yard, or elsewhere. Whenever the puppy wanders up to the trainer, or any person for that matter, it should be greeted with a big welcome. The puppy can be taught more formal recalls at six to seven weeks of age by the trainer attaching a long line to the puppy's collar. The trainer lets the puppy run around in its own little world and then calls it by name, at the same time gently pulling the puppy in and praising it from the time it is called, with a big fuss and lots of praise when it reaches the trainer. About six times at any session is sufficient.

Although puppies become a little uncooperative at about 12 to 16 weeks, the same format continues. Remember, *never call a puppy to you and punish it.* Catch it in the act and go to the puppy immediately. When the puppy or adult comes when it's called it must be rewarded.

If the puppy is inclined to be mischievous when left to its own devices and enjoys a dig in the garden or spreading newly washed clothes around the yard, simply don't allow the puppy the opportunity to

do these things. Place it in a pen, tether it or keep it under foot and keep an eye on it. Prevention is the easiest method until the puppy matures. Remember you have an active toddler on your hands and puppies love adventure as much as the human child.

Puppies love to chew, particularly when teething, so provide them with some doggie toys. Nylabones®, Gumabones®, and Plaque Attackers® all come in a variety of shapes, colors, and sizes, and provide the puppy with hours of chewing that is not only fun, but good for its teeth. If the puppy is discovered with something it is not allowed to chew, quietly praise the puppy at the same time removing the object and replacing with its own toy and continue the praise. If the puppy is reprimanded the trainer can cause himself problems should he wish to teach the puppy to retrieve. It will soon understand that it can only chew its own toys.

As with adult dogs, food tidbits can be given from time to time but not on a regular basis. The puppy must learn to do things to please the trainer, not do things because it is bribed.

Housebreaking is easily achieved by taking the puppy outside straight after a sleep, meal or drink of water, and at frequent intervals in order to avoid an accident. When it goes to the toilet repeat a particular word to the puppy (such as "toily"), at the same time verbally praising it, and in time it will learn to obey nature on that command word. If the puppy messes inside scold it verbally and repeat the above process, even if by this time it has no desire to empty its bladder or bowels, it will soon learn what is required of it.

Don't rub the puppy's nose in the urine or feces, it serves no purpose at all.

Puppies can be introduced to some formal type training such as the exercises given later in this book from eight or nine weeks but only for a few minutes, definitely no more than five minutes at a time, putting the pressure on at about five months of age.

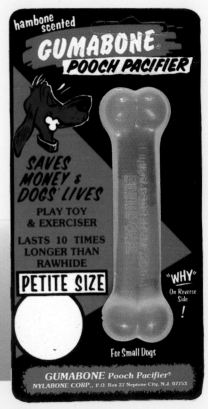

The Puppy Bone® from Nylabone® is the "standard" nylon bone to begin a puppy with.

The Gumabone® is made of polyurethane and is softer than the Nylabones®. Many puppies prefer Gumabones® because they are softer and taste and smell good.

The Plaque Attacker Bone™ from Nylabone® has raised dental tips that help fight plaque on the dog's teeth. These are superior pacifiers as well as excellent dental devices. Nylabone® products are the safest and most cost effective of all dog bones available to dog owners today.

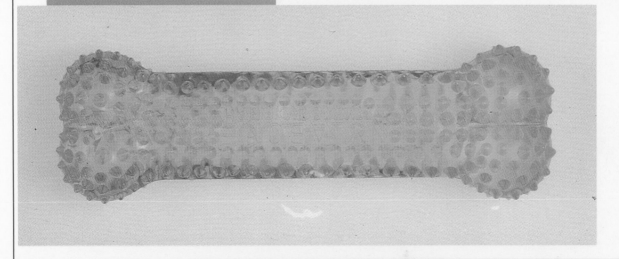

THE DOG'S
POINT OF VIEW

Before we venture on to the practical lessons, I wish to undertake an imaginary exercise putting you—the trainer—in the dog's shoes, so to speak. Pretend that you're a very young child and one of your parents takes you to a large sideshow. You're surrounded by wonderful things that are driving your young inquisitive mind wild—there are knock 'em downs with fluffy toys to win, ice cream treats, fairy floss, dagwood dogs, show rides, and animal shows with all the noises and colours that excite the young mind. Imagine the scene: there you are, a young child amongst all this delightful activity, then this parent decides you have to sit down and do your schoolwork. Frustrating? Of course it is.

There are people everywhere having fun and you've got to work on your maths. Hard to understand in your young mind? Do you think you would rebel, or at least display some resistance for a time?

All right, lets take another scenario. Your first lesson with your dog. You take him to a nearby park, there are children playing on monkey bars and swings who are shouting, squealing, and laughing. In another direction there is a group playing touch football, running and chasing, laughing, and making exciting noises. There are two dogs running loose, urinating on trees and posts marking territory, and nearby there is heavy traffic passing by with all the associated noises and interesting smells. You're in that park with dog attached to lead and check chain. Bearing in mind that he has the inquiring mind of a young child, he is surrounded by people running, shouting, laughing, traffic noise, dogs to challenge, and territory to claim. He has a sense of hearing at least six to eight times more acute than ours, and a sense of smell at least one million times stronger than ours.

The dog is at his own sideshow but he has one

Incorrect use of check chain. The chain is through the bottom of the ring and will lock when checked during training.

problem, you keep giving him a command with a word he doesn't understand and keep walking in the opposite direction he wants to go. He wants to run over and check the strange dogs, join the kids, and chase the football. But he has a problem, you keep checking his desires by tugging on the lead whilst continually repeating this strange word. It becomes a contest—he doesn't want to sit down and do schoolwork. He decides to rebel and makes a determined effort to check out the sideshows. Then the battle between dog and trainer begins in earnest.

Should the dog be a type 1 you will have had your clash of wills but you would have slowly brought the dog around to your way of thinking. If the dog is a type 2 it will have made you the laughing stock of the park as you virtually engage in combat with a stubborn, arrogant specimen of "man's best friend." The dog will have pulled you around the park totally ignoring your commands, which later turn to pleadings as you become more embarrassed and frustrated. A type 3 dog will finish the training with you strongly in need of

sedation as the dog aeroplanes around you in blind panic and doing somersaults. People will have accused you of ill-treating your dog as you leave the park cloaked in embarrassment.

As the trainers of types 2 and 3 dogs return home they usually vow and declare that they will never be embarrassed by a dog again. They often blame themselves as they have read literature telling them how easy it is to train the family pooch and of the

Jeffrey and Beau demonstrate the correct use of the check chain: the chain is dropping through the ring.

rewards and pleasures for their efforts. What went wrong, you ask? You followed the instructions in the books and it sounded easy, right? Well, the fact is that dogs are as different as people, and their training has to be approached accordingly.

It is very hard to replace the instruction and guidance of an experienced

instructor, however I'll presume that you don't have this advantage during the course of this book.

By this time you will have a fair idea of which category your dog falls into. You may find that you have placed your dog in the wrong category as time goes on—a type 1 dog may in fact be a type 2 dog and vice-versa. In any event, make the assessment to the best of your ability and get on with the training. Dog training, like anything else, is a series of experiences made up of success and failure. So don't be disappointed if you make mistakes, just be quick to rectify them.

Take the check chain as per the photograph, place it over the dog's head and attach the lead.

QUIET LOCATION

Take the dog to a quiet location, whether it be in the backyard or an isolated public area. You're looking for an area with a minimum of distractions— you are avoiding taking the dog to a sideshow.

Remind yourself that you have many months of patient training ahead of you, and that the dog may not be particularly easy to train. Relax and forget the day's problems—it is not a battle of man versus beast. It is simply you involving yourself in a project of training your dog in basic obedience exercises.

STAGE ONE:
INTRODUCTION TO HEEL EXERCISE

Put your right hand through the loop of the lead and take up about 12 inches of lead, grasping it with the right hand also. Leave the left hand free to praise and for repositioning the dog when you commence training the exercises. You will now be standing near your dog with about four feet of loose lead.

The dog is not placed in any particular position, so you just walk off in any direction you wish. At this point you're simply teaching the dog to walk with you without it pulling on the lead. We will get more exacting in five day's time. No command is given because it is not a specific exercise in that the dog is being taught good manners by not pulling you around the park.

As soon as the dog pulls away from you, stop walking and stay where you are. When the dog is at the full length of the lead, pull the lead abruptly back towards you, bringing the dog to a sudden halt. Don't drag the dog back to you—just halt his progress. If necessary use the left hand to assist the right hand.

Wait until the dog stops pulling, then continue walking and halting the dog sharply every time it dashes to the end of the lead to investigate something. He can learn to investigate at the end of a loose lead without pulling you from pillar to post.

Walk at a slow pace, stop to correct the dog, then continue in a slow pace. Throughout this process you remain calm and in control.

A type 1 dog will turn and look at you for communication after a few times, questioning your actions. When it looks at you make sure you look directly into the dog's eyes and talk quietly and pleasantly to it. After a moment proceed on and every time the dog faces you after the sudden correction establish eye contact and praise.

The session lasts ten minutes and each time the training ceases you will sit with the dog for a period of about 30 minutes, giving it a "down" or "quiet" time.

When the dog pulls away from you, stop and pull back abruptly on the lead. Then wait until the dog stops pulling and continue walking.

This quiet time allows the actions of the training session to soak into the dog's brain, and is preconditioning the dog for the stay exercises by teaching it to settle itself.

Whilst sitting with the dog make sure to sit in a chair or on a fence so that you're above the level of the dog. If you sit on the grass with the dog he will think of you as being on his level and want to play.

During quiet time, be sure to sit on a fence or chair so that you're above the level of the dog.

Don't let the dog play with your hand or run around your seat. Insist that it stays settled and should it become unbearable with hyperactive behaviour grab it behind the neck and rough it, while at the same time giving it a verbal thrashing with a very convincing display of outrage at its behaviour. The words you use don't matter, simply tell it off. Bear in mind that you're developing your talents as an actor with the dog, so that when it settles down you change from a person of outraged demeanour to the quiet firm parent of an errant toddler. Quietly praise to show the dog that all is well when it stops its rude behaviour and controls itself.

The training sessions can be conducted up to four times a day, with the training taking place for four days.

If you are training a type 2 dog expect to be in for a frustrating four days. In some cases you may find that you don't have a type 2 dog at all, but a type 1 dog who was simply in need of reminding that you're around and you insist on being shown respect.

The trainers of type 2 dogs will have to get more forceful with the corrections after the first session, halting the dog and leaving no doubt in its mind that you're not going to be pulled around by some rude, ill-mannered canine companion whom you feed and care for at some considerable expense.

Type 3 dogs are a worry due to their timid state of mind. In the case of dogs that are timid because of unfortunate breeding, you can only try your best and my best wishes go to you. I've trained numerous dogs of this type with very good results in some cases while others were simply beyond help.

When I think about dogs who have had their spirits broken and the end result that can be achieved, it brings me to mind of a R.A.A.F. Police Dog called Pedro. Pedro had his spirit broken by a handler clearly unsuitable to be given the responsibility of an animal. At this time a chap who became a legend in the R.A.A.F. Police Dog Mustering due to his freakish ability as a dog trainer—Cpl. Nev Kershaw—-advised young airman Jeff Woods to accept Pedro as his partner and persevere with him. Pedro's psychological state was such that when Jeff attached a lead to Pedro, the dog's response was to cringe and urinate in fear.

Jeff was fortunate in passing from Kershaw's influence to the guiding hands of another outstanding dog handler in the form of Sgt. Bruce Stevenson—a gentleman who was to become my dog training role model.

In 1971 a particularly astute gentleman in the form of Flt. Lt. Bill Perrett, founder and Officer in Charge of the R.A.A.F. Police Dog Mustering, set about on his annual man-dog team assessments throughout Australia, Malaya and Singapore. The highly esteemed Perrett Award for the top man-dog team that year was won by Lac. Woods and Police Dog Pedro.

Some type 1 dogs are forced into the type 3 category due to erratic and moody owners, particularly if the dog is highly strung with a strong will to please. Indeed it is not uncommon to find these tragic specimens on the verge of a nervous breakdown due to mental cruelty. Police Dog Pedro was such a dog only he had the misfortune of suffering physical cruelty as well. However, to witness Jeff and Pedro going through their paces in obedience, tracking, attack work, obstacles, and repertoire of dozens of tricks, not only would a person never dream of the previous mental condition of the dog, but it was clearly evident that the emphasis on bonding between dog and handler elevated Jeff to a height rarely reached by most dog trainers in any field.

Simply put, Jeff and Pedro became so much in love with each other they were virtually psychically linked. The high standard of training achieved from there was a credit to Jeff's determination and self-discipline. His goal was to train his dog to be of the

Your bond with your dog gives him confidence. Here Christopher and his best friend Quattro are sharing time between training sessions.

highest standard possible in this field and his dedication and persistence were unwavering.

The emphasis is on bonding and you, as the trainer and normally owner, will have to give the dog confidence. You must make the dog your best and closest friend.

Remember eye contact. When your dog looks directly at you, never turn away.

Bear in mind also that quite a lot of dogs, particularly small breeds, are trained to be timid. Dogs are quick to manipulate owners and the dog soon learns that if it shows fright at something unexpected, the owner immediately picks it up, taking great pains to soothe the frightened little dog. This type of dog is also often the one that becomes very aggressive if it doesn't get its own way around the house, even to the extent of snapping at the owner if an attempt is made to remove it from a chair or the bed.

It is also not uncommon to see dogs unintentionally trained to be frightened of thunderstorms, gunfire, and fireworks. This has happened when the puppy was startled at the sharp sound and the over-concerned owner quickly picked it up, doing an overkill on reassuring it that mummy or daddy was there and there was nothing to be frightened of.

Type 3 dogs are trained the same as 1 and 2 at this point. Communicate only when the dog comes close to you. Should it pull away from you in a blind panic or roll around on the ground in submission, ignore it for a couple minutes then start off again. Do not, at any time, speak to the dog either to sympathise with it or praise it until it stands quietly near you.

There is no time limit of four days on type 3 dogs with this exercise. Continue for several more days if necessary, until the dog is content to walk along near you without resisting.

SUMMARY OF STAGE ONE

You're standing in a stationary position in the training area with about four feet of lead hanging loose, then set off walking in a slow pace. Should the dog pull away from you straining at the end of the lead, stop suddenly and snap back on the lead, stopping the dog in its tracks. Do not continue walking until the dog stops pulling; only pat and talk to the dog when it returns to you. Remember eye contact; when the dog looks directly into your eyes, you look directly into its eyes. No more than four sessions a day, ten minutes at a time, with 30 minutes quiet time.

STAGE TWO:

CONTINUING INTRODUCTION TO HEEL EXERCISE

After the fourth day it is time to extend the training session to 30 minutes. Again a maximum of four sessions per day with a half hour quiet time in order to let the dog absorb the lesson and teach it to remain settled. This also continues for four days.

During the course of the fifth to eighth day, instead of walking then stopping to check the dog, you walk in a deliberate line from point A to point B to point C and so on. An easy way is to sight up a tree or some object, make that point B, then walk straight towards it. Should the dog pull out, check the dog as before then continue walking to point B, etc.

Apart from the aspect of walking in straight lines on day five, if the dog is not walking close to you, then a sharper correction is applied when you halt to stop the dog walking away from you. The more the dog ignores you the greater the force is used when checking the dog.

By the eighth day the trainers of type 1 should have their dogs walking close to them with about four feet of lead hanging loose. By virtue of the lead being slack means the dog is walking with the trainer because: a) it knows it will get checked when the lead is pulled taut; and b) the dog has learned to be content with the trainer's companionship.

The trainers of type 2 will fully realise that they have a problem child on their hands. They will be

Correct the dog by making a right turn away from the dog, stepping off on the right leg, and continue walking in a straight line. Demonstrated by Christopher and Nikita.

Step quickly to your right—away from the dog—and release the slack in the lead. Then snap the lead sharply across your body.

experiencing frustration caused by the arrogance of the dog and its determination to pull the owner where it pleases. Type 2 trainers will have to be people of a particularly determined nature and the harder the dog pulls, the harder the correction.

Type 3 trainers may commence this new procedure even if the dog is still exhibiting slight signs of fear. Continue to walk slowly from point to point, stopping when the dog becomes unsettled, and praising only when the dog comes and remains beside them.

Remember to keep calm and be patient.

SUMMARY: STAGE TWO

Walk at a slow pace from point to point in a straight line, stopping only to check the dog when it takes up the slack in the lead and pulls away. Check the dog, praise, then continue in the straight line.

Top left: **The correct way to hold the lead for the heel exercise.**

Top right: **Christopher and Nikita demonstrate the correct heel position.**

Bottom Left: **Give the command heel and step off on your left foot, as demonstrated by Ryan and Cassie.**

Bottom right: **Whenever the dog falls in correctly by your left side, pat the dog with your left hand and praise it.**

STAGE THREE:
HEEL EXERCISE

The heel exercise, apart from the stays, is probably the most important exercise due to the fact that you are teaching the dog to pay attention to you. You cannot learn anything unless you're paying attention, and a dog won't learn anything unless it is paying attention to you.

On the ninth day we commence teaching the dog to walk close by your left side with its head level or slightly in front of your left leg. No more than four training sessions a day for a period of ten minutes with 30 minutes quiet time.

Take up extra slack in the lead, leaving a distinct loop between you and the dog. The command "heel" is given in a clear, moderate voice, with a distinct inflection. In other words, say the word "heel" exactly the same way every time. Each of the command exercises will have a different tone to each command word. The voice inflection must not be harsh or aggressive, but clear and firm. Be careful not to sound like you're rousing on the dog.

For the next four days the command "heel" is given every time you make a positive correction to the dog, teaching it to associate this particular word with your insistence that it must come to your left side.

On the ninth day set about walking in a straight line to point A, giving the heel command and stepping off on your left leg at a normal pace. When the dog tries to change direction and pulls the lead taut—remember there should be four feet of loose lead if the dog's standing beside you—step quickly to your right away from the dog while at the same time releasing the slack in the lead already held in the right hand and snap the lead sharply across your body.

As you step to your right

The correct position for the stand, parallel with your body, viewed from the front.

and correct the dog, continue walking at a normal pace in the same direction you're facing and head directly for a new point.

The correct stand position with the dog parallel to your body and the chest level with your knees.

Alternately correct the dog by making a right turn away from the dog (stepping off on the right leg) and continue in a straight line. Whenever the dog dives away from you and pulls the lead taut, repeat the procedure.

When the dog is walking nicely with you so that the lead is slack, manipulate the dog to your left side by simply steering it with the left hand, taking the lead and wheeling it into position (the lead is still held with the right hand). When the dog is in position, pat with the left hand and verbally praise whilst continuing to walk.

Whenever the dog falls in correctly by your left side, continue walking but also pat with the left hand and praise at the same time. Should the dog show resentment at this procedure and back up on the lead defying you, continue walking and drag it along with you. The dog will soon realise that you hold the lead and it will follow. As soon as it reaches your left side, praise it.

The trainers of type 1 will have little difficulty with this exercise. However, if you have a type 2 dog you can expect a number of reactions. It may continue to ignore you, pulling away from you to go and investigate trees and things; it may act like a hooked game fish, pulling back and rearing on its hind legs and throwing itself on the ground; or it may even threaten you with a growl and perhaps a nip on the back of your leg. Regardless of its resentful behaviour, totally ignore the dog, continuing to step to your right and correct it. Most dogs who exhibit aggression do no more than that, and will fall into line when it is ignored and not spoken to, or patted when it falls in by your left side.

If you're training a type 2 dog and it has been particularly infuriating throughout the session, totally ignore it during the 30-minute quiet time. It will ignore you for a period of time, but it will eventually want a chat and try to attract your attention. Turn your face away from it, averting your eyes, and continue giving it the cold shoulder treatment until the next training session. This method has worked well for centuries with women who were offended by their menfolk, and it works very well for a lot of dogs.

After 12 days it may

become apparent that your type 2 dog is beyond your capabilities at this time. However, all is not lost. Go back to day nine's training schedule and repeat for two weeks, also including stage four, where we include the stand exercise. If you don't make progress after this time you will have to face the fact that you need help in the form of an experienced trainer, or perhaps your veterinarian can recommend a professional training establishment.

A word of caution when selecting help, however. Professional trainers now abound in the more populated areas, and many have no qualifications other than self-recommendation. Choose one who has extensive previous practical experience in the police, prisons or military-type areas, or one who was/is a successful competitor in the obedience trialing or Schutzhund areas. These people will be happy to provide evidence of their achievements in the form of certificates issued by legitimate organisations.

It must be remembered, however, that some type 2 dogs are very aggressive—to the point of being dangerous. This behaviour

A problem dog in the hands of a competent trainer can make successful strides.

can be caused by owners who have been cruel to the dog or indeed, too soft with a dog who has an inherent dominant and aggressive nature. These dogs can usually be trained successfully if they are placed in the right hands.

Moreover, some dogs, like some people, are quite simply born bad for whatever reason and are extremely dangerous to

Your professional trainer may not have the experience of this author, but you can judge to see that he has had success with many dogs in your area.

both yourself and the general public. The only solution with these dogs is to have them put down.

The type 3 dogs may not be ready for stage three at this point, however if you're satisfied that your dog is sufficiently settled, proceed on. Bear in mind to keep the corrections light. Remember that it is best to go too soft at first as you can always make the corrections harder later.

SUMMARY: STAGE THREE

Step off on the left leg at the same time saying the command word "heel." Walk in a normal pace directly towards point B in a straight line. When the dog pulls away from you step to your right, away from the dog, at the same time releasing the extra lead held in the right hand, repeating the word "heel," and continue walking in a straight line. Or, turn right by stepping forward on the right leg and walk to a new point. When the dog comes to your left side pat with left hand and give oral praise. No more than four sessions a day with 30 minutes quiet time.

Before commencing stage four, give the dog two days' spell from training.

STAGE FOUR:

STAND EXERCISE

On day 15 you continue training stage three. However, we now introduce the stand exercise by your left side. The dog is brought to a halt beside your left leg as you come to a halt, its body is straight and parallel to yours with the dog's chest level with the front of your leg. This exercise is included with the heeling exercise and the session is for 15 minutes with 30 minutes quiet time. Train for five days then rest for two.

A problem encountered by people training types 2 and 3 is that once their dogs are taught to sit, it can be difficult to teach them to stand. The easy way to solve the problem is to teach the dog to stand first.

I also hasten to add that the stand exercise is one that dogs often regress on. This can be rather frustrating unless you understand that you can train your dog for a considerable period of time with it reliable in the stand position, then it suddenly forgets how to stand on command. If this happens to you further along the track, simply retrain stage four. Remember, dogs get mental blocks just like people.

Not only is teaching the dog to stand very easy, but you can also introduce a hand signal for this exercise right from the start.

Whilst heeling the dog and it is walking nicely by your left side, give the command "stand" in a clear, distinctive voice and in a different tone to the heel command. At the same time, with your left hand, make a semicircle or windshield wiper motion in front of the dog's eyes from left to right, stopping a little past the dog's head with palm facing towards the dog's eyes, fingers outstretched and pressed together.

All right, now picture

Step One *(left)*: Give the command stand and use a windshield wiper motion in front of the dog's face (starting from the left). **Step Two *(right)*:** Move the hand across the dog's face to the left.

Step Three *(left)*: Bring your hand back along the dog's side and stop its forward motion by propping him in front of his left rear leg.
Right: Forewarn your dog by giving the command and hand signal so as to avoid confusing your dog when you halt. Take one extra step before halting.

this: you're walking along with the dog, waiting until it is in the heel position by your left side, and you're still walking. Now come to a halt and as you do, give the stand command and at the same time give the hand signal with the left hand. As your hand goes from right to left, immediately bring your left hand back along the dog's left side, propping its forward movement by blocking the dog's left hind leg. Hold this position for three or four seconds then give the command "heel," walking the dog forward to continue the heel exercise and praising it at the same time. Don't grab a handful of skin and hair at the dog's flank—it's painful and some dogs may bite your hand on reflex. If this should happen it will serve you right.

In this session go through your normal heeling exercise and every so often place the dog in the stand position for about six times per session.

You now only use the heel command as you start the session, and you use the heel command each time you heel the dog off from the stand position.

SUMMARY: STAGE FOUR

Carry out your normal training routine practising the heel exercise. When the dog is in the correct heel position as you're walking, give the

command "stand" while also giving the hand signal with the left hand and prop the dog's left rear leg, halting the dog. Hold for three or four seconds, then give the heel command and walk off, praising the dog. Five or six repetitions of the stand exercise each session is sufficient. Each time you heel off from the stand repeat the command heel.

No more than four sessions a day, 15 minutes at a time with 30 minutes quiet time. Train for five days then rest for

two.

A little further down the track you will teach the dog the automatic sit; that is where you're heeling the dog then coming to a halt with the dog sitting at your left side without a command.

When you halt, the dog will be in the process of sitting. However, when you give the stand command the dog will have to get back up. To avoid confusing the dog, simply forewarn the dog of your

Sitting is not the most natural position for a dog. Praise the dog when he is in this position.

intention to give the stand command by giving the command, then take an extra pace before halting.

For example: You're walking along at a normal pace with the dog in the heel position at your left side, you say "stand" and give the hand signal at the same time, and take an extra pace before stopping. This procedure also applies under the same circumstances with the drop exercise.

STAGE FIVE:
SIT EXERCISE

After the rest period you continue training stages three and four. However, we now introduce the sit exercise by your left side. The dog is brought to a halt by your left side with the backside on the ground and front legs in an upright position. Its body is straight and parallel to yours with the dog's chest level with your leg. This exercise is included with the heeling and standing exercise and the session is for 15 minutes with 30 minutes quiet time. Train for five days then rest for two.

Start your training session with a few minutes heeling in order to get the dog's mind on the job, then give it about six stand exercises. This is simply repetition of previous exercises of course, but repetition is vital to the dog's learning progress.

Now to teach the sit, simply continue to heel the dog until it is in the correct position, then as you come to a halt take up the lead short in the left hand, transferring to the right hand so that the right hand has about one foot of taut lead from the end of the check chain. Give the command "sit" in a different voice inflection to the heel and stand commands. At the same time hold the dog's head up with the lead while you push its backside down with your left hand.

You will find that it is easier to execute if you commence this procedure just before you come to a halt as the dog is still beside you. Once you stop and then attempt the procedure, the dog will probably be moving forward and you then have to bend forward to sit the dog. You will not only find this awkward but the dog is not learning to associate this new word with sitting beside you.

When you have sat the dog make sure that it is sitting squarely on its backside with both hind legs upright (not splayed).

If the dog sits with his backside out and he is too heavy for you to handle, take a step forward and steer him into the correct position.

Step One (left): To teach the dog to sit as you come to a halt, take up the lead short. As you start pulling up on the lead, bring your left hand over the dog's backside. **Step Two** (right): Pull up on the lead and push down on the dog's backside until he is sitting.

Letting the dog slouch over in the sit position not only looks untidy, but it will be more inclined to lay down when you reach the stage of doing sit-stays.

I was quickly chastised years ago by the then-Flt. Sgt. Tom Daley and Sgt. Bruce Stevenson. The point made was that lazy habits are quickly formed and hard to break and a strong work ethic was essential right from the start. A piece of advice I have never forgotten and greatly appreciate to this day.

There is no hand signal on this occasion—only the voice command.

Should the dog sit with its backside away from you or behind you, simply reach down with the left hand and maneuver the dog into the correct position (straight and parallel to you). If the dog is large and too heavy for you to manhandle, take a step forward on your left leg and steer the dog into position.

All right now picture this: you give your dog the command to heel and walk off continuing this exercise for a few moments, then give the dog about six stands. Now you practice the procedure of sits about six times. Remember, each time you start off after completing a stand or sit exercise, give a fresh heel

Lift up the dog's head and practice eye contact. Never forget to praise your dog.

exercise, only put the dog in the sit position for a few seconds before placing it in the stand position. Remember to praise the dog before recommencing the heel exercise.

When praising the dog in the sit position, practice eye contact. Lift the dog's head up, lower your face to the dog's and look directly into its eyes as you give a few seconds of warm, affectionate, verbal and physical praise. Your dog should be settled in the stand exercise by this time so that you can carry out the same form of praise.

AUTOMATIC SIT

As a result of sitting the dog numerous times over the first few weeks the dog will be totally familiar with the exercise. Simply stop giving the verbal command, and when coming to a halt lift the lead up, indicating to the dog to adopt the sit position. This is normally sufficient, however should the dog be a little arrogant give it a light open-handed slap on the area above the tail as you come to a halt.

For example: you're walking along in a normal pace with the dog at your left side in the heel position and when you come to a halt the dog should sit without command or assistance.

command. When you have completed the sit exercise, bring the dog to its feet by pulling the lead forward, taking the dog up and at the same time giving the hand signal and command "stand," propping it there. Hold him there for five to ten seconds, then give the heel command and walk him off.

What we are doing is teaching the dog not only to sit, but also the stand exercise in relation to its new position.

As with the stand

SUMMARY: STAGE FIVE

Heel the dog for a few minutes, getting its mind on the job. Practice the stand exercises. Give the dog about five or six sits, praising before giving the heel command to walk off. Follow the procedure of giving the dog a sit command, then put the dog in position, followed by a stand exercise. Keep the dog in a sit position for a few seconds before changing to heel or stand. Increase the time period for the stand position to five to ten seconds. Concentrate on close eye contact whilst giving verbal and physical praise. By the end of the training session you should have given the dog about 12 stands and about 12 sits.

No more than four sessions a day, 15 minutes at a time, with 30 minutes quiet time; five days training with two days' rest.

COMMON PROBLEMS

At this point you may find that the dog is inclined to walk forward of your body in the stand exercise rather than standing with its chest level with the front of your left leg. This may be solved by balancing on your left foot and bringing your right foot up and placing it

If your dog is walking forward of your body in the stand, balance on your left foot and bring your right foot up in front of the chest, as shown by Ross and Robyn.

Left About-Turn

While walking your dog in the heeling exercise, pivot around following your left shoulder, which will result in you turning into your dog. Simply pass your lead from your right hand to your left hand, at the same time wheeling the dog around to your left side as you continue walking back along the same path. Praise as you continue walking.

> **Right turn: If the dog is not paying attention, give a sharp snap with the lead and continue walking.**

quickly in front of the dog's chest, sharply propping it in the correct position.

You will find that if the dog's feet are in line with your left heel when you bring it to a halt in the stand or sit position, the dog's chest will be level with your left leg.

EXTEND THE HEEL EXERCISE

Introduce right, left and about turns whilst heeling the dog.

Left Turn

While walking the dog in the heeling exercise, make a sharp left turn and continue walking. Should the dog be in your path don't walk around it—walk through it and push it out of the road with your legs. The dog must learn to work around you, not you work around the dog.

Right Turn

While walking the dog in the heeling exercise, make a sharp right turn away from it and continue walking. Should the dog be caught napping and is left behind, give it a sharp little pull with the lead and keep walking, praising the dog as it catches up.

> **Left turn: If the dog is in your path, push it out of the way with your knee.**

Right About-Turn

While walking your dog in the heeling exercise, turn around on the spot following your right shoulder and walking back on the same path, with the dog coming around in the turn with you still on your left side. Praise as you continue walking.

SIT-STAY EXERCISE

After the rest period continue training stages three, four and five. However, we now introduce the sit-stay exercise, where the dog will be taught to sit and remain in position so that you can walk off and leave it behind. This session lasts for 15 minutes with 30 minutes quiet time. No more than four sessions a day. Five days' training and two days' rest.

Commence your training routine with the usual heel exercise for a few moments to get the dog's mind on the job, then the routine of about six stands, six sits, six sits then stands.

With the sit-stay we now introduce a new hand signal to be given at the same time as a verbal command, and this is achieved by using your left hand, with fingers outstretched and pressed together. Position the dog in a sit and give the dog the verbal command "stay" with a different voice inflection from the other commands. At the same time place your left hand in front of the dog's eyes,

blocking its vision for a second or two, then almost immediately step in front of the dog with the right leg leading. Turn quickly so that you are facing the dog and remove your hand from in front of the dog's eyes. You will be so close to the dog you will almost be standing on his toes.

From the dog's point of view: it has been placed in the sit position, it then hears a word spoken from you that is both unfamiliar in sound and tone as its vision is blocked. Before it can twist its head so that it can see, you have removed your hand and it finds that your standing in front and facing him.

Lean down and verbally and physically praise the dog, remembering eye contact. Stay there for about five seconds then step quickly back to your previous position beside the dog, continuing the praise. Should the dog

attempt to stand (remember, the lead is held in the right hand), raise it upward while at the same time leaning forward and pushing its rear end down into the sit position with the left hand, repeating the command "stay."

As with all the exercises it takes practice to carry out the procedures smoothly and methodically, so don't get unsettled. Just plug away in a patient, determined, and workmanlike manner, reminding yourself that you're working with the

The correct sit position, chest level with your knees and parallel with your body, demonstrated by Ryan and Cassie.

The correct sit position, viewed from the front, demonstrated by Ryan and Cassie.

the lead up with the right hand and pushing the dog's backside down into the sit position with the left hand. After about ten seconds quickly step back into position beside the dog and praise again. Repeat this procedure about six times, gradually increasing the time period in front of the dog to 60 seconds, and extend the distance between you and the dog up to the end of the lead. No more than four sessions a day 20 minutes at a time, with 30 minutes quiet time. Train for five days then rest for two.

COMMON PROBLEMS

You may find that the dog appears reluctant to sit although it will have the message by now. If this is the case, instead of pushing the dog's backside to the ground, give it a sharp open-handed smack to the area above the tail while forcing the dog to sit. As a result of the unexpected force the dog will usually respond quickly.

Should you also find the dog slow when you're stepping off or doing the right turn in the heeling exercise, hold the lead in your right hand and drive your left knee through the lead, consequently propelling the dog forward with you.

equivalent of a toddler.

After your first effort, stay by the dog's right side for about ten seconds, quietly praising the dog and letting the experience soak into its brain, then repeat the procedure. Do this six times.

Over the next five days slowly work your way to the end of the lead so you will be standing three or four feet in front of the dog. Also extend the time period whilst in front of the dog so that by the end of the first five days you will be standing in front of the dog for at least 60 seconds or longer.

SUMMARY: STAGE SIX

Complete a few minutes of heeling, including the turns, then go through the routine of stands, sits, sits, then stands. Put the dog in the sit position beside your left leg, give the verbal command "stay" as you block its vision at the same time, then step around to the front of the dog leading on the right leg, and turn to face it. Lean forward and praise the dog. Correct it if it stands up by extending

STAGE SEVEN:

INTRODUCTION TO RECALL EXERCISE

steps backward, coming to halt, and praise the dog in a gay, somewhat excited voice, encouraging it to return swiftly to you. When it reaches you, tell it to sit, leaning down and sitting the dog so that it is facing you with the body in a straight line.

After the rest period, continue training stages three, four, five, and six. However, we now introduce the recall exercise, where the dog will be taught to come to you when it's called and sit in front of you. This session lasts for 20 minutes with 30 minutes quiet time. Train for five days then rest for two. No more than four sessions a day.

Step One: When you're heeling, suddenly step backward and quickly take five or six steps. At the same time say come and praise the dog so that he comes to you.

As usual, practice heeling exercises for a few minutes to gain the dog's attention. Now whilst walking the dog, suddenly start stepping backwards quickly so that the dog overshoots and has to turn around and run towards you. As you start peddling backward, call the dog's name followed by the command "come."

Take about five or six

Step Two: When the dog reaches you, lift up the lead and push down on the dog's backside.

From the dog's point of view: the dog is walking along concentrating on you in case you make a sudden turn in any direction, when it suddenly feels that you're not beside it. The lead suddenly becomes taut,

Step Three: The dog is now sitting in front of you, praise your dog as demonstrated.

causing the dog to turn towards you. At the same time it hears its name and a new word in a new voice tone.

The dog's initial reaction is one of confusion but when it finds that it is being praised in a happy voice it enthusiastically runs toward you. The dog then hears the familiar command "sit," but before it becomes confused (because it is not at your left side), it feels the lead

lift upward. You're leaning down pushing its backside to the ground with the other hand. The dog is baffled by all this sudden rush of events but by immediately praising it and it seeing your eye contact

and happy, smiling facial expression, the dog feels good about this event and remains relaxed.

You will find that the dog will enjoy this exercise and start to watch you more carefully as a result.

Continue this procedure about six times, sandwiching it in between the other exercises.

From this procedure you will teach the dog that when you say "come" it must run toward you and

sit in front of you.

When the dog is in the correct position and you have completed the praise, pivot around in an about-turn so that you're facing in the same direction as the dog. At the same time give the command "heel" and walk off, praising the dog as it catches up on your left side. The come command must be given in an inviting tone to encourage the dog to come to you quickly and willingly.

SUMMARY: STAGE SEVEN

Walk along heeling the dog, then suddenly start walking backward, taking about six quick steps. As you do so, pull the lead taut, drawing the dog back to you. As the lead pulls taut, call the dog's name and give the command word "come" in a pleasant, inviting tone of voice. When you come to a halt facing the dog, tell it to sit, raising the lead upward with the right hand leaning over to sit the dog with the left hand. Praise for about five seconds, then give the command "heel" and do an about-turn, walking off with the dog and continuing to praise. The session lasts for 20 minutes with 30 minutes quiet time. Train for five days then rest for two. No more than four sessions a day.

STAGE EIGHT:

DROP EXERCISE

After the rest period continue training stages three, four, five, six, and seven. However, we now introduce the drop or down exercise. The dog is to be taught to lay flat on its belly, back straight with hindquarters upright (not slouched over) in a position called the sphinx position. (Remember the carved animals on the Egyptian tombs?) This session lasts for 20 minutes with 30 minutes quiet time. Train for five days then rest for two. No more than four sessions a day.

A hand signal may also accompany the drop command by using your right hand. Start with fingers outstretched and pressed together with palm facing the dog's eyes. Then take your right hand from in front of the dog's eyes and extend toward the ground.

Practice verbal and hand signals together so the dog learns the commands. Then practice using voice only, or hand only, to provide more variety in the dog's training.

To achieve the sphinx position simply reach down and pull the offending leg (the one under the dog) out from under it, thus straightening the dog's back. If the dog is being difficult in this area wait for a week after the dog is dropping well and start again.

Commence training the dog with a few minutes of heel work, walking in a straight line, left and right turns, and left and right

Step One *(left)*: To drop your dog, give the command drop and, using your right hand as shown, make a downward movement in front of the dog's eyes toward the ground. **Step Two** *(center)*: Take your dog down into the drop position. **Step Three** *(right):* When your dog is in the correct position, you stand up as demonstrated.

The first method to get your dog to drop, pull slowly down on the check chain and click your fingers, motioning toward the ground.

The second method for the drop, if the first method fails, is to apply downward pressure at the base of the neck and pull the dog's legs forward bit by bit until he is on the ground.

about-turns.

Mingle the other exercises doing some sits to stands, sits, recalls, stands, and sit-stays. Avoid doing the exercises in any particular order at this time, remembering that dogs get bored doing obedience work in the same old routine.

The drop is an easy exercise if your dog is a type 1 or 3 dog. A type 2 dog however, will display a variety of reactions from just plain old, "I'm not going down," and gritting the teeth at the same time, to others who will attempt to bite the trainer.

Dominant dogs view this exercise as a submissive act and are not happy about being made to lay down even if you are the owner or trainer and the bond is strong. But obedience training is about discipline and you're the pack leader who must be obeyed.

Regardless of what type category your dog is, introduce the exercise in a soft manner and get harder if it's necessary.

METHOD ONE

Place the dog in the sit position by your left side. Kneel down so that your head is close to the dog's head. Give the command "drop" in a soft, encouraging tone of voice, and at the same time pull down slowly on the check chain with the left hand as you click the fingers of your right hand, motioning toward the ground. The dog won't associate the command to a required response initially like the other exercises, but if it goes down for you praise and let it up after a few seconds, continuing the praise for a few more seconds. Heel the dog off for a moment or two, repeating the procedure about six times.

Your aim at this time is simply to teach the dog to lay down on the word "drop" as downward pressure is applied to the check chain. If method one doesn't work, try method two.

METHOD TWO

Place the dog in the sit position by your left side. Kneel beside the dog with your head close to the dog's head. Hold the check chain at the top of the dog's neck with the left hand. Apply downward pressure with the left hand as you move the dog's front legs forward bit by bit until it is laying down. Stay with the dog, praising it, and let it up after a few seconds continuing the praise for a few more seconds. The dog may stand up as soon as you start pulling the front legs forward. As soon as the dog stands up, you stand up as well (you've then gone from the level of an equal back to a level of dominance). Command the dog to sit in a firm, aggressive tone, pushing its backside down immediately. This teaches the dog that your manipulation of its front legs doesn't entitle it to change its position. Repeat the above steps and if you're successful, stay with the dog praising and let it up after a few seconds, continuing the praise for a few more seconds. Heel off for a few moments and repeat the procedure about six times.

METHOD THREE

Should the dog still be determined to stand you may try food inducements. Position yourself as per method one with a tempting food treat in your right hand. As you say "drop," move the food from close to the dog's mouth down towards the ground, encouraging with verbal praise. The dog may jump up to grab the food or snap at it rather than go down. Do not let the dog take the food; it only gets the reward when in the drop position. Persevere with about six attempts. Should the food inducement prove effective, use for three days then wean out on the fourth and fifth day, so that the dog is only getting a reward every second drop on the fourth day, and every third drop on the fifth, with no food in the subsequent training sessions.

You will usually find that within a few days after the food has been withdrawn, it will refuse to go down.

Step One *(left)*: A third method for the drop is to straddle the dog, sitting on his rear and grasp his front legs. **Step Two** *(above)*: Lift the front legs forward and force him down under your body weight.

The fourth method for the drop, if the former three methods have proven ineffective, is to try tempting him down with food. Do not give him the food until he is lying down.

Don't go back to the food, for the dog is dictating the terms like a gangster—no pay, no work. You have achieved your aim of communicating the message of the exercise to the dog, now you revert to your role as the pack leader and go back to method two.

Still no success?

Don't despair, it does happen quite often. People who have never trained a dog other than type 1 will never understand the frustration of training a very stubborn type 2. If you're roundly criticised by

If all else has failed, here is the fifth and final method! If the dog is aggressive, stubborn, or otherwise unmanageable, try cajoling him down in a peaceful fashion.

these people, simply invite them to take the dog and train it for you; they may not find it so easy, either.

The dropout rate of beginners in obedience clubs is higher than 50% after the first four months, mainly because of type 2 dogs who refuse to cooperate with the trainers, causing them embarrassment and heartbreak despite their hardest efforts. So, keep your chin up with the drop problem and keep trying.

After you have completed the five-day procedure, return to your normal training program, positioning your dog in the drop from the sit position. From there you may heel the dog off, bring it back up into the sit position after giving the sit command, or straight into the stand after giving the stand command. When the dog is dropping from the sit position, start dropping it from the stand position, and also dropping the dog whilst heeling.

Vary the exercises—don't get into a set routine.

SUMMARY: STAGE EIGHT

Remember it is better to start too soft than to start too hard in your training (generally) and this applies

with the drop exercise. Therefore commence with method one and work through to method three if necessary.

Common Problems

You will probably find that the dog will be reluctant to drop promptly, in which case you put the dog in the sit position, give the dog the drop command, then grasp the lead close to the check chain with the left hand forcing the dog down to the ground. This method can also be applied

when you start teaching the dog to drop as you're walking it along in the heel position.

Dogs are great compromisers at the best of times and there is no exception with the drop. Some dogs will often lay almost to the ground and wait patiently for you to push them down; they don't mind the correction because they're getting attention. If this should happen go to the next method.

To illustrate a common problem: once your dog understands the drop but becomes reluctant, grasp the lead close to the neck and force the dog down.

If your dog likes to compromise and gets you to bend down each time, give a push on the lead with your foot as shown here by Ross and Daisy.

STAGE NINE:

EXTENDED SIT-STAY EXERCISE

Now position the dog in the sit-stay with you at lead's length in front of the dog. Return to the dog by walking around it past the dog's left shoulder and halting at the dog's right shoulder. Pause for three or four seconds before praising.

From there you can give the dog another exercise, such as drop, stand, heel off, or another sit-stay.

The dog must be taught to lock itself in position as you walk back to it and around it. Should the dog move out of position, correct it immediately by putting it back in position and chastising it with your voice.

When you have cemented this message in the dog's brain, take a wooden stake, tent peg, a piece of reinforcing rod or similar object for the purpose of driving it in the ground. Place the end of the lead over this object to secure the dog until it is reliable enough to do away with the peg.

Drive the peg into the ground. Positioning your dog in the sit beside your left side, place the end of the lead over the peg. Give the

Step One *(left)*: To teach your dog the sit-stay exercise, place your left hand in front of the dog's eyes. Step Two *(center):* While holding your hand in front of the dog's eyes, quickly step in front of him. Step Three *(right)*: Turn quickly so you are facing your dog and remove your hand, as shown by Ross and Robyn.

normal command to stay and walk off from your dog for a distance of five paces, then turn and face the dog, watching to see if it breaks. If the dog breaks, return straight to it, chastising it in a stern voice and put it back in position, then praise to indicate what you want.

Go back to your original position facing the dog and continue with the previous procedure when necessary, making the dog stay for about two minutes. Build up to five minutes by the end of the five-day training period.

As time passes and the dog becomes more reliable, walk further away from the dog until you reach the stage where you can leave the dog in the stay off the peg and do other things, such as washing the car, gardening or sitting down to read a book.

Remember, dogs have no powers of reasoning for the purpose of training so think for your dog and break down the training step by step.

Break down the stay exercise into two parts; part A returning to the dog and part B actually walking around the dog to its right side.

With the above principle in mind remember your eye contact. When you return to the dog, look at it—it will look at you for communication so why look anywhere else than directly at the dog? If it breaks put it back in position. When you're returning to the dog, adopt a relaxed manner— not an aggressive attitude that threatens the dog in the event it moves. Give a couple of quiet words of praise as you return to let the dog know that so far it has been doing what you want of it. If the dog moves, go to it and correct it immediately. As you halt beside the dog's right shoulder, pause for a few seconds then praise.

Sit- and drop-stays are very important, not just because they are useful exercises, but also because they teach the dog self-discipline in that it must learn to control itself (e.g., it cannot run off and chase a dog or cat because it would like to). The dog learns that it must do as it's told by the pack leader.

Over the coming weeks extend the dog's time period for a sit-stay to at

Left: **If your dog attempts to stand when he is in the sit-stay position, raise the lead and push his backside down.** *Right:* **In heel work, if your dog is slow when you are stepping off or doing a right turn, drive your knee through the lead.**

Step One *(left):* **When you return to your dog on the stay, walk past his left shoulder... Step Two** *(center):* **.... around behind the dog... Step Three** *(right):* **...and halt at his left shoulder, as demonstrated by Cassie and Ryan.**

least ten minutes.

I realise that dogs in obedience trials are not required to sit-stay for this period of time, but any well-trained police or military dog would be expected to stay for a longer period of time as they are working dogs—not dogs trained for a sport. Moreover, it is the working dog ethic on which I have based this book.

Once you have commenced training your dog in the extended stay exercises, whether it be sit, drop or stand, you no longer need to use the quiet time at the end of each training session. Instead, finish the session with a game for a few minutes to lighten it up, such as fetching a ball.

To extend your stays so that your dog cannot run away if he breaks, drive a stake into the ground and drop the loop of the lead over it.

STAGE TEN & ELEVEN:

DROP- AND STAND-STAY EXERCISES

STAGE TEN: DROP-STAY

The training of the drop-stay is the same as the sit-stay in stage six and stage nine. The only difference being that the dog is allowed to relax and lay with its hindquarters no longer in the sphinx position.

STAGE ELEVEN: STAND-STAY

Again, the training of the stand-stay is the same as the sit- and drop-stays. However, the dog is often tempted to walk forward as it is already on its feet. Simply correct and the dog will soon get the message. Three minutes maximum is sufficient time in this exercise.

SUMMARY

When you commence sit-stays off the lead, reduce your actual heel work routine (heel, sit, stand etc.) to ten to 15 minutes per session. Increase the time period for sit- and drop-stays, extending them up to ten minutes each exercise from time to time. Stand-stays need be no longer than three minutes duration—it's an exercise that isn't used as often as the others. Stays can be performed whilst you're doing some housework, washing the car, etc. Be alert to the dog breaking its position so you can return to it promptly and reposition it. Don't forget eye contact. Praise as you return and when you complete the exercise.

The stand-stay is demonstrated here by Aleisa and Charmayne.

The drop-stay is accomplished the same as the sit-stay.

STAGE TWELVE:
RECALL EXERCISE

In this exercise you are teaching the dog to come when it's called on the command "come" from a distance. This exercise can be commenced after the dog will sit-stay reliably off-lead. No more than six times a session.

Sessions are now about 15 to 20 minutes with extra time allowed for the stay exercises. Quiet time is now replaced with a play time.

Again, remember the principle that a dog has no powers of reasoning for the purpose of training so think for your dog and break down the training step by step.

Break down the exercise into four parts. In part A the dog is in a stay position regardless of whether it be sit, drop, stand, or running

Step One *(top left)*: To teach the dog the recall (come when called), put the dog in a stay and turn to face it at the end of the lead. **Step Two** *(bottom left):* Give the command come and pull on the lead. **Step Three** *(top right):* As the dog arrives, pull up on the lead and push down on the dog's backside. **Step Four** *(bottom right)*: The dog sits nice and straight in front of you, as shown by Ross and Nikita.

free. Part B is the dog returning to you. In part C the dog is sitting in front of you. Part D is finishing the exercise with the dog coming around your right side and behind you, sitting on your left side.

Step One *(left)*: To finish the recall exercise, give the heel command and take a step forward on the right foot. **Step Two** *(left center)*: Pull the dog around behind you, changing the lead from your right to left hand. **Step Three** *(right center)*: Now step forward on your left leg and bring the dog to your left side. **Step Four** *(right)*: As you halt, sit your dog as shown.

heel (the command heel is used on two occasions—this is the second). You now take a step forward on the right foot, stopping near or past the dog's right rear leg. At the same time pull the dog to your right side, bringing it around behind you to your left side and passing the lead from the right hand to the left hand behind your back as you step forward on your left leg, taking an extra pace or two if you wish. As you halt, give the dog the sit command, sitting the dog beside you, and praise generously.

You have already taught the dog to respond to the command "come" and made the exercise an enjoyable experience for the dog. Now:

PART A

Put the dog in the sit-stay for a start. Let the dog walk away to the end of the lead and turn to face it. The dog waits until you're ready to call it. Before calling always vary the time period (i.e., five or ten seconds, whatever suits you). Dogs have a built-in clock and will anticipate if you use the same time period. Say the dog's name softly. If it moves forward correct it and teach it to stay until

the command "come" is given. Give the dog's name softly, pause for three or four seconds, then give the command "come" in an inviting tone and pull on the lead indicating for the dog to run to you.

PART B

As the dog runs in, praise.

PART C

Lift the lead up indicating for the dog to sit in front of you. At the same time give the command "sit." Don't give physical praise until the dog has sat correctly in front. When satisfied, reach down and pat, never forgetting eye contact.

PART D

To finish the exercise take the lead in the right hand. Give the command

As the dog becomes cooperative in part D change the procedure.

While the dog is sitting in front of you, take a step back on the right foot. At the same time bring the dog around your right side and up beside your left side as you step forward on the right leg, bringing the dog in line with your left leg.

The left leg doesn't move.

As the dog gets the idea, start lengthening the distance between yourself and the dog from ten paces to 15 paces, etc., until you can set the dog up at one end of a football field and call it.

If the dog should prefer to go for a wander rather than come to you, attach a

Step One *(left)*: Advanced finish. Take a step back on the right foot and at the same time pull the dog with you.
Step Two *(center)*: Change the lead to your left hand and bring the dog around as you step forward on your right foot.
Step Three *(right):* Sit your dog as shown.

long cord such as a clothesline to the dog's collar and pull the dog in.

The dog must be conditioned that it can

never get away with shooting off on you and this can be achieved by constant control.

Should the dog be slow, it will come to you more willingly if you clap the front of your thighs and run backward a few paces to excite the dog, and display a big fuss when it reaches you.

Step One *(left)*: If your dog is slow to come in on the recall, bend down and clap your thighs as you call him. **Step Two** *(right):* Sit your dog in front of you, as shown by Aleisa and Nikita.

REVIEW

We have now covered the six basic exercises. It's time to start extending your dog by taking it to a variety of strange training areas, continuing to apply the training principles. Most dogs will get a little excited at the sideshows, but stay relaxed and persevere.

A normal training session at this point should go something like this: heel the dog for a few moments, incorporating all the turns; give the dog sits, drops, and stands; and work the dog's up and down in these positions beside you, remembering that variety stops both yourself and the dog from getting bored.

Do a series of recalls varying the distances between you and the dog, possibly finishing with a three-minute stand-stay, five- to ten-minute sit-and/or drop-stay. No more quiet times required, however a game for a few minutes to brighten the dog is desirable.

Usually about this time trainers are inclined to almost drop the praise, expecting the dogs to perform like robots. Remember to keep up the praise and eye contact—it is imperative.

You may find that the dog will regress on some exercises due to new distractions or mental blocks at times. If you have a problem with an exercise, take the dog back to its early training steps and patiently run through them again.

The dog is not normally the problem—you are. You may be too soft or too hard, or perhaps you haven't broken down your training enough and you're confusing the dog.

Repetition, praise, correction—always be consistent.

The dog has no powers of reasoning for the purpose of training so break down your exercises step by step to avoid confusing the dog.

Find some time to train your dog most days of the week, even if it's only ten minutes a day when you're on a busy schedule.

Got a training problem? Look in the mirror and you will find the solution.

If this dog has a training problem, he is looking directly at the cause of it. The trainer is always responsible: Never blame the dog. Good luck!